EXPLORING THE SUBATOMIC WORLD

Understanding
PROTONS

B. H. Fields
and Fred Bortz

Cavendish Square

New York

To Alex, with every positive wish.

Published in 2016 by Cavendish Square Publishing, LLC
243 5th Avenue, Suite 136, New York, NY 10016

Library of Congress Cataloging-in-Publication Data

Bortz, Fred, 1944- author.
Understanding protons / Fred Bortz and B.H. Fields.
pages cm — (Exploring the subatomic world)
Includes bibliographical references and index.
ISBN 978-1-50260-546-7 (hardcover) ISBN 978-1-50260-547-4 (ebook)
1. Protons—Juvenile literature. 2. Particles (Nuclear physics)—Juvenile literature.
I. Fields, B. H., author. II. Title. III. Series: Exploring the subatomic world.

QC793.5.P72B68 2015
539.7'2123—dc23

2015003670

Editorial Director: David McNamara
Editor: Andrew Coddington
Copy Editor: Cynthia Roby
Art Director: Jeff Talbot
Designer: Stephanie Flecha
Senior Production Manager: Jennifer Ryder-Talbot
Production Editor: Renni Johnson
Photo Research: J8 Media

The photographs in this book are used by permission and through the courtesy of:
MARK GARLICK/Science Photo Library/Getty Images, cover; Monika Wisniewska/
Shutterstock.com, throughout; DeAgostini/Getty Images, 7; Universal History Archive/
UIG/Getty Images, 8; Welcome trust/File:'Distillatio', scene in an alchemist laboratory
Wellcome M0018149.jpg/Wikimedia Commons, 10; Georgios Kollidas/Shutterstock.com,
11; chemistryland.com/File:Gaylussac.jpg/Wikimedia Commons, 13; Thomas Forget,
14; SSPL/Getty Images, 17; Magnetix/Shutterstock.com, 18; Thomas Forget, 20; Thomas
Forget, 23; George Grantham Bain Collection (Library of Congress)/File:Ernest Rutherford
LOC.jpg/Wikimedia Commons, 24; Kurzon/File:Gold foil experiment conclusions.svg/
Wikimedia Commons, 26; Trambitskiy Yury/Shutterstock.com, 27; Thomas Forget, 30–31;
Thomas Forget, 32; Elliott & Fry/Hulton Archive/Getty Images, 35; Keystone/Getty Images,
37; Bernard Miller/NASA, 40; MASIL Imaging Team/NASA, 43; Jon Brenneis/The LIFE
Images Collection/Getty Images, 45; David Levenson/Getty Images, 45; Thomas Forget,
47; NASA's Goddard Space Flight Center, 49; Jupeart/Shutterstock.com, 50; Rob Atkins/
Photographer's Choice/Getty Images, 51; Reactor- Sean Gallup/Getty Images, 53.

Printed in the United States of America

Contents

Introduction

W hat is matter? That is one of oldest questions in science. It is also among the most productive, because as we learn more about matter, we also find new questions.

For example, you probably know that every substance on Earth is made of **atoms** and combinations of atoms called **molecules**. But do you know what makes hydrogen different from nitrogen? What makes carbon different from silicon? What makes what makes any one kind of atom different from any other?

The scientific theory of atoms goes back to 1803, when John Dalton (1766–1844) adopted an idea of the ancient Greek philosophers Leucippus and Democritus. Twenty-three centuries earlier, long before modern science, they imagined cutting up a piece of matter until it was *atomos*, meaning indivisible.

Dalton used that notion of indivisible particles to interpret laboratory observations. In Dalton's theory, the atoms of Leucippus and Democritus turn out to be molecules. A water

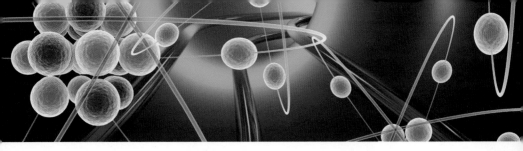

molecule is made of two hydrogen atoms and one oxygen atom, and is therefore not indivisible. But it is the smallest unit of matter that can still be called water. Dalton spoke of **elements**, which are made of only one kind of atom, and **compounds**, which are made of only one kind of molecule.

Dalton's theory still considered atoms indivisible, but as more scientists discovered more elements, it was natural to wonder if the atoms were made of even smaller particles that distinguished one kind of atom from another. By the end of the nineteenth century, physicists (scientists who study matter and energy) began to discover those subatomic particles. And in the early twentieth century they realized that one of the most important of those was the **proton**.

This book is the story of how protons were discovered, where our understanding of protons has led us, and what lies ahead.

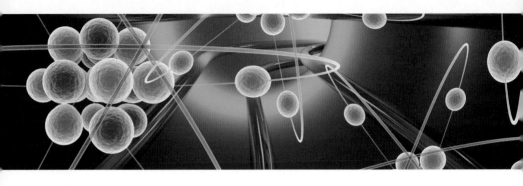

1 ATOMS,
Molecules, and Matter

The ancient idea that matter is made up of tiny, indivisible pieces has led scientists in directions that Leucippus and Democritus could never have imagined. Today's world of human-made substances depends on our knowledge of atoms, the subatomic particles within those atoms, and the forces that hold them together or break them apart.

Those ancient Greek philosophers began with two simple questions: What is matter made of, and why do different kinds of matter behave so differently from each other? When they imagined dividing everyday substances into smaller and smaller bits until the pieces were indivisible atoms, they also decided that the atoms of each substance would have a particular shape and texture. For instance, they concluded that water atoms would be round and smooth, while rock atoms would be hard and sharp or gritty.

The presumed atoms were much too tiny for the Greeks to test their ideas. Besides, the notion of testing theories by observation, a cornerstone of modern science, was not yet part of human culture. Toward the end of Democritus' life, Greek philosophy entered what is often called a "golden era," where great thinkers such as Socrates, Aristotle, and Plato used their powerful minds and logic to deduce what they believed to be the truth about the natural world.

Aristotle was so brilliant in many fields that his ideas were rarely questioned. For nearly two thousand years, most people accepted his conclusion that all the world's matter was made of four elements: earth, air, fire, and water. The idea of atoms all but disappeared. Today we know that both Democritus and Aristotle were right in general but wrong in detail.

Democritus. This sculpture depicts Democritus, the founder of an ancient Greek philosophical movement known as atomism. He proposed that matter is made of tiny indivisible particles, an idea that eventually led to the modern theory of atoms.

Democritus spoke of a limit to how small a piece of matter can be cut and still remain the same substance. That idea was right, but most substances are compounds and mixtures, not elements. The smallest possible piece of

Aristotle's Elements. Atomism was largely abandoned for nearly two thousand years and replaced by the four elements of Aristotle: earth, air, fire, and water. This illustration from the Middle Ages shows the symbols for those elements plus a fifth, aether, which was thought to make up the heavens.

most substances is usually a molecule instead of an atom. Furthermore, molecules can be divided into their atoms, and even atoms are not indivisible.

Aristotle was correct that all matter is made of combinations of particular elements, but not the four he wrote about. Water is a compound, earth and air are mixtures containing both elements and compounds, fire is a process that produces energy as atoms rearrange themselves into different compounds, and the number of natural elements is nearly one hundred, not four.

As you might imagine, the road from the philosophy of the ancient Greeks to today's scientific knowledge of atoms is a long one with many interesting twists and stops along the way. It begins with an activity called **alchemy**, in which people tried to make certain substances out of others, often by heating things together. Most often, alchemists were searching for ways to turn less valuable metals into gold using techniques that we now know were doomed to failure. Gold is an element, and neither ancient alchemy nor modern chemistry can change one kind of atom into another.

Though many alchemists were fraud artists, others succeeded in developing a rudimentary knowledge of matter, extracting or purifying many useful elements and compounds from natural substances. By the seventeenth century, scientific thinking had begun to take hold, and alchemy was gradually transformed into the science of chemistry. Eighteenth-century chemists made a number of important discoveries, including facts about the behavior of gases, the processes of combustion and corrosion, and the relationship between electricity and matter. None of those phenomena were fully understood, but plenty of evidence and measurements were being gathered systematically and scientifically.

An Alchemist's Laboratory. This drawing by sixteenth-century Flemish painter Jan van der Straet shows one of alchemy's most common practices: distillation. This remains a common technique for separating substances in modern chemistry and industry.

As the nineteenth century dawned, English scientist John Dalton (1766–1844), already in his thirties, was turning his attention from meteorology to chemistry, hoping to gain a better understanding of the gases of the air. He soon realized that the ancient idea of atoms could explain many of the phenomena that others had observed in gases and chemical reactions. In 1810, Dalton published a book that revolutionized chemistry. Titled *A New System of Chemical Philosophy*, the book was based on the assumption that all matter was made of atoms.

Dalton explained that each element was made of a particular kind of atom, and all of its atoms were identical to each other. He also wrote that atoms of different elements have different properties, including their weight. When atoms join to form compounds, it is always in small numbers of whole atoms—no fractional atoms allowed.

John Dalton (1766–1844). Dalton is considered the father of modern chemistry for his 1810 breakthrough book that introduced the concepts of elements, compounds, atoms, and molecules.

Discovering that Water is H_2O

How did scientists discover that a water molecule is formed from two hydrogen atoms and one oxygen atom—which gives it the chemical formula H_2O? They did so by running experiments with combining gases.

In 1808, French chemist Joseph Louis Gay-Lussac (1778–1850) described what happened when two gases reacted to form another gas. From performing numerous experiments, he found that the volumes of the reacting gases at the same temperature and pressure were always in the ratio of simple whole numbers. For instance, when hydrogen burned in oxygen to form water, for every 2 cubic meters (528 gallons) of hydrogen burned, it took 1 cubic meter (264 gal) of oxygen. The result was 2 cubic meters (528 gal) of water vapor. He proposed that discovery as a law of nature.

When Italian scientist Amadeo Avogadro (1776–1856) read about Gay-Lussac's proposed law of gases, he tried to understand why that could be so. When he thought about the nature of gases in containers, he envisioned lots of molecules colliding with each other and with the container walls. Because the molecules were so far apart, it didn't matter what kind of molecules they were. He concluded that any gas having the same temperature and pressure and occupying the same volume had the same number of molecules. In 1811, he proposed that as a law of nature.

Combining the two laws, it became clear that Gay-Lussac's law of whole number volumes was also a law of whole number of atoms or molecules. Thus a molecule of water had to contain two

Joseph Louis Gay-Lussac (1778–1850). French chemist Gay-Lussac discovered that the volumes of gases reacting at the same temperature and pressure are always in the ratio of small whole numbers. He proposed this as a law of nature.

hydrogen atoms and one oxygen atom. Other experiments showed that hydrogen molecules were two hydrogen atoms combined, or H_2, and, likewise, oxygen molecules were O_2. Therefore Gay-Lussac's experiment showed this reaction:

$$2H_2 + O_2 \longrightarrow 2H_2O$$

(2 hydrogen molecules and 1 oxygen molecule
produce 2 molecules of water)

Using those simple rules, Dalton was able to determine the **atomic mass**, or **atomic weight**, of different elements. He assigned hydrogen, the lightest element, one unit of atomic weight, and determined the atomic weight of other atoms from that. For instance, he knew that water was a compound of hydrogen and oxygen, with eight times as much oxygen by weight. Assuming that a water molecule had one atom of each element, he set the atomic weight of oxygen at eight units. Later on, when more research showed that water molecules had two atoms of hydrogen and one of oxygen, scientists corrected that result, setting the atomic weight of oxygen at sixteen.

Following Dalton's method, scientists studying chemical reactions gradually identified more compounds and the elements that composed them, and they determined the atomic weights of each element. Though no one had detected individual atoms, Dalton's idea of elements and compounds, and atoms and molecules, had given chemistry a new basic vocabulary. As is often the case with scientific

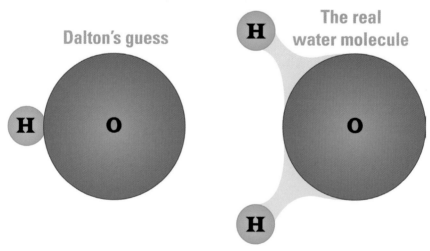

Close, but Incorrect. By assuming water was a compound of one hydrogen atom and one oxygen atom, Dalton drew the incorrect conclusion that the atomic mass of oxygen was eight. Later experiments showed the correct formula was H_2O, and thus the atomic mass of oxygen was sixteen.

breakthroughs, atomic theory also opened up a wealth of new questions, including: How many elements are there, and is there a way to classify them to better understand their chemical behavior?

Mendeleyev and the Periodic Table

By 1869, a total of sixty-three elements were known, and scientists were having a hard time keeping track of them. They could see hints of similarities and patterns among the elements, such as in their melting or boiling points, their densities (how much each cubic centimeter weighs), the way they combined with other elements, and the properties of the compounds they formed. Still, no one had come up with a successful way to classify them—until Russian chemist Dmitry Ivanovich Mendeleyev (1834–1907) had a dream.

Mendeleyev was a professor at St. Petersburg University, known for his thorough knowledge of the elements and their properties. He also owned a small country estate, and his neighbors relied on his advice about farming and cheese making. So from time to time he would schedule a visit to the country. Traveling by train, he would often occupy his mind by playing "patience" with a deck of cards. Like most solitaire games, the object of patience was to build an arrangement of the cards from the highest to the lowest within each suit (spades, hearts, diamonds, and clubs).

Before one such trip in early 1869, Mendeleyev had been working continuously for three days, trying to discover a way to classify the elements that would make sense of all the fragments of patterns he and others had noticed. He decided to make a set of cards, one for each element, listing the known properties of each. He arranged them in order

Some Elements Discovered by 1869

Mendeleyev's periodic table was built on many centuries of discovery. Here, in alphabetical order, are some of the elements he knew well.

Aluminum (Al): Discovered in 1825 by Hans Christian Oersted in Denmark.

Boron (B): Discovered in 1808 by J. L. Gay-Lussac and L. J. Thenard as well as Sir Humphry Davy.

Calcium (Ca): Discovered in 1808 by Sir Humphry Davy in London, England.

Carbon (C): Discovered in prehistoric times.

Hydrogen (H): Discovered in 1766 by Henry Cavendish in London, England.

Iron (Fe): Discovered by ancient civilizations.

Lithium (Li): Discovered in 1817 by J. A. Arfwedson in Sweden.

Nitrogen (N): Discovered in 1772 by Daniel Rutherford in Edinburgh, Scotland, as well as in the early 1770s by Carl Wilhelm Scheele in Sweden, Henry Cavendish, and Joseph Priestly in England.

Oxygen (O): Discovered independently around 1772 by Carl Wilhelm Scheele in Sweden and 1774 by Joseph Priestley in England.

Zinc (Zn): Known in India and China before 1500 and to the Greeks and Romans before 20 BCE.

Tabelle I.

Typische Elemente

H							
			K = 39	Rb = 85	Cs = 133	—	—
			Ca = 40	Sr = 87	Ba = 137	—	—
			—	?Yt = 88?	?Di = 138?	Er = 178?	—
			Ti = 48?	Zr = 90	Ce = 140?	?La = 180?	Th = 231
			V = 51	Nb = 94	—	Ta = 182	—
			Cr = 52	Mo = 96	—	W = 184	U = 240
			Mn = 55	—	—	—	—
			Fe = 56	Ru = 104	—	Os = 195?	—
			Co = 59	Rh = 104	—	Ir = 197	—
			Ni = 59	Pd = 106	—	Pt = 198?	—
H = 1	Li = 7	Na = 23	Cu = 63	Ag = 108	—	Au = 199?	—
	Be = 9,4	Mg = 24	Zn = 65	Cd = 112	—	Hg = 200	—
	B = 11	Al = 27,3	—	In = 113	—	Tl = 204	—
	C = 12	Si = 28	—	Sn = 118	—	Pb = 207	—
	N = 14	P = 31	As = 75	Sb = 122	—	Bi = 208	—
	O = 16	S = 32	Se = 78	Te = 125?	—	—	—
	F = 19	Cl = 35,5	Br = 80	J = 127	—	—	—

der chemischen Elemente.

The First Periodic Table. This diagram shows Russian chemist Dmitry Mendeleyev's first published periodic table of the sixty-three known chemical elements at that time. Later research discovered additional elements that fit into some of the gaps in this chart and had properties very similar to Mendeleyev's predictions.

of increasing atomic weight. Just before he was to leave to catch his train, the weary professor fell asleep and dreamed of playing patience with his deck of element cards. When he woke, he knew what he had to do. The atomic weights were like the order of the cards. All he needed was to figure out how many groupings there were (nature had no reason to choose four suits like in playing cards) and how many cards were in each.

By the time Mendeleyev arrived at his destination, the arrangement had begun to fall into place. Though he had used other properties to develop his arrangement, he discovered that the groupings seemed to follow a chemical property called "valence." Valence accounted for how many of one atom

would combine with how many of another. For example, the elements called the alkali metals—lithium, sodium, potassium, rubidium, and cesium—all fell into alignment, as did the elements called halogens—fluorine, chlorine, bromine, and iodine. As atomic weight would increase, the atoms would follow a pattern: going from one valence to the next to the next, and periodically starting over again. Mendeleyev thereby called his arrangement the **periodic table of the elements**.

The table was not perfect, and it had a few gaps. Mendeleyev claimed that the gaps represented elements not yet discovered. He predicted not only that they would be found, but also what compounds they would form and what their atomic weights, density, and other properties (such as melting or boing points) would be. Mendeleyev was right, and with those discoveries, the periodic table of the elements was established as one of the great ideas of chemistry.

Mendeleyev's discovery of the periodic table is considered one of the great achievements of science. But it was far from a complete description of the nature of matter. It led to many important new questions, especially this one: What makes the properties of atoms periodic? Answering that would require the discovery of subatomic particles.

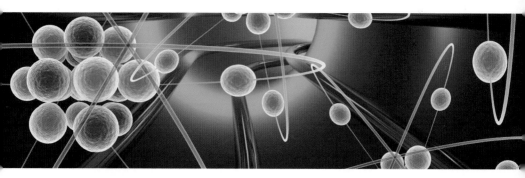

2 DISCOVERING
the Nucleus

After Mendeleyev published the first periodic table, chemists continued to discover new elements, and they continued to have the properties that Mendeleyev predicted. It was clear that he had found more than a useful arrangement of the elements; he had found a fundamental aspect of matter. Something caused elements to have periodic properties. But what was that something? And did it have anything to do with Dalton's atomic theory?

Scientists were willing to say that matter behaves as if it is made of atoms, but many were still looking for proof that atoms actually existed. Then along came J. J. Thomson (1856–1940) of Cambridge University in England, who in 1897 described his discovery of tiny bits of matter that he called corpuscles and we now call **electrons**.

By then, scientists understood electricity quite well. They knew that two positively charged bodies or two negatively

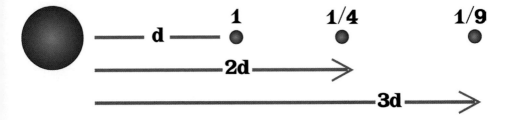

The Law of Electrical Forces. By the end of the nineteenth century, scientists recognized that chemistry and electricity are closely related. They used the law of electrical forces, illustrated here and described on this page, to determine in 1897 that the newly discovered electron had a mass that was much smaller than the smallest atom. That made it the first known subatomic particle.

charged bodies would repel (push away) each other, while a pair of bodies with opposite electric charges would attract each other. The attractive or repulsive forces get much stronger as the charged bodies get closer together. Decreasing their separation to half its value multiplies the force by four (2 × 2). If the distance is shortened to one-third of its original value, the force increases by nine (3 × 3).

They also knew that electricity was related to chemical reactions and valences, and thus it was probably important in atoms. Thomson's corpuscles had unexpected properties. They carried negative electric charge and were less than a thousandth as heavy as the lightest atom, hydrogen. (We now know that a hydrogen atom is about 1,800 times as heavy as an electron.)

Yet despite that huge difference in mass, the corpuscles carried as much negative charge as a hydrogen atom might carry in its most positively charged state. That result suggested that atoms are not indivisible but are made of even smaller subatomic particles—tiny negatively charged electrons and much heavier positively charged particles—held together by electric forces.

Evidence of Atoms

Still many scientists felt that atomic theory was incomplete without evidence of actual atoms. The problem was that they weren't looking in the right places. The evidence that atoms and molecules were real was already known but was not recognized. It was called **Brownian motion** after the English botanist Robert Brown (1773–1858), who observed in 1827 that pollen grains suspended in water under a microscope followed random jiggling paths, even if the water was absolutely still.

Over the years, some scientists proposed that these grains moved because they were bumped about by molecules, and others studied Brownian motion more carefully, measuring the paths for different-sized particles at different temperatures. Finally, in 1905, Albert Einstein (1879–1955) calculated the motion that would be expected if atoms moving at a certain temperature collided with dust or pollen particles of a certain size, and the results matched Brownian motion perfectly. People couldn't see individual atoms, but they could see their effects.

Rutherford's Surprise

If atoms were real and contained tiny negatively charged electrons, what about the positively charged parts? Since atoms are electrically neutral overall, they must contain as much positive as negative electric charge. Scientist wondered if that positively charged matter was in the form of the individual particles or as a spread-out mass. J. J. Thomson put forward an educated guess. Since electrons carry so little mass, he envisioned the positively charged bulk of atoms as a kind of pudding containing tiny electron plums.

Brownian Motion

This illustration shows what Robert Brown observed when he followed the movement of pollen grains suspended in water through his microscope in 1827. Instead of staying in place or slowly drifting, the grain abruptly changed direction at random intervals.

At first, Brown suspected the movement was because the grains had come from living things. So he tried it with pollen from dead plants. The movement was the same. Then he tried tiny bits of fossilized wood. Finally he tried material that had never been alive—bits of window glass and dust from a stone from The Great Sphinx. No matter what he tried, the particles followed similar random, jerky paths.

Brown tried to explain the phenomenon in various ways: There were currents in the water due to evaporation; there were tiny vibrations that he couldn't feel; it was due to the light striking the particles so he could see them. Yet none of these were satisfactory.

In the 1860s and 1870s, physicists studying thermodynamics began to suggest that the motion might be due to water molecules colliding with the grains. French scientist Léon Gouy (1854–1926) repeated the experiments with different liquids and under different conditions. He showed that the motion was not affected by strong light or **electromagnetic** fields. That strengthened the idea that molecular collisions were the cause. Finally, in 1905, Albert Einstein's calculations matched the observations so well that no one could deny that Brownian motion was indeed the result of collisions with the fluid's molecules.

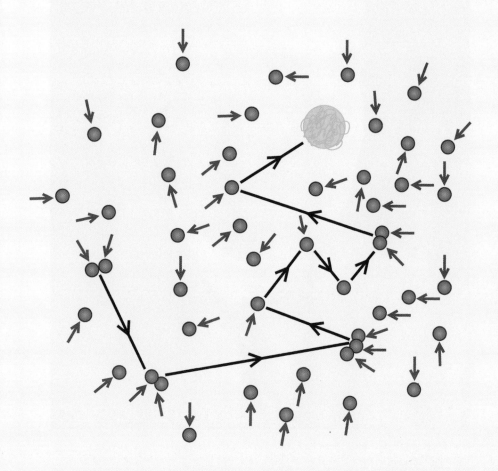

Brownian Motion. In 1827, botanist Robert Brown observed an odd phenomenon under his microscope. Pollen grains suspended in water followed jerky, irregular paths, even when the water was perfectly still. Other scientists looked at other particles, including those that were never associated with a living organism, and found similar motion. They began to suspect that it resulted from random collisions with water molecules. Calculations by Albert Einstein in 1905 matched observed results. It was the first direct evidence that atoms and molecules exist.

Ernest Rutherford (1871–1937). Rutherford, already a Nobel Prize winner for his work with radioactivity, used alpha particles to probe the internal structure of atoms and found a surprising result. Most of an atom's mass and all of its positive electric charge was in a tiny central region called the nucleus.

Thomson's plum pudding model was put to the test by Ernest Rutherford (1871–1937), who had come up with a way to probe matter by bombarding it with the **emissions** from radioactive substances. Rutherford was one of the first scientists to explore the **radioactivity** as Thomson's student at Cambridge between 1895 and 1898. There he found two distinct forms of radioactivity, which he named "**alpha rays**" and "**beta rays.**"

He then went on to become a professor at McGill University in Montreal, Canada, where in 1902, he and his colleague Frederick Soddy (1877–1956), discovered a third form of radioactivity they called "**gamma rays**." They also discovered that alpha and beta radiation were streams of fast-moving particles of opposite electric charge. The alphas were positively charged and much more massive than the negatively charged betas. (We now know that beta rays are electrons.)

Rutherford returned to England in 1907 as a professor at the University of Manchester and began shooting beams of **alpha particles** through metallic foil and measuring how the alphas deflected, or scattered, as they interacted with atoms of the metal. By studying alpha **scattering** carefully, he hoped to be able to determine the size, spacing, and perhaps even the shape of the atoms in the foil. His student Hans Geiger (1882–1945) devised an instrument to detect and count the alpha particles. They determined that alpha particles were helium atoms without their electrons, just as Rutherford had suspected.

In 1909, they began their scattering experiments, and the results were surprising. Nearly all the alphas passed straight through the foil or deflected only slightly. If the atoms were hard balls, Rutherford and Geiger would have expected more deflection. Also puzzling was this: a few alpha particles were unaccounted for. Geiger's counters had been placed behind the metal foil. Had some particles been deflected so much that they had missed the detectors? If so, what was scattering those few alpha particles through such large angles?

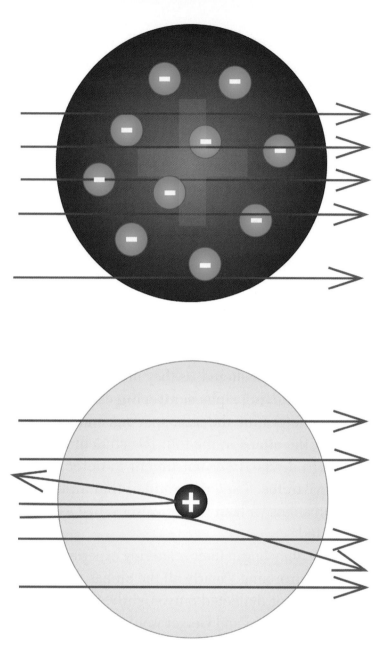

The Proof Is in the Not-Pudding. Rutherford's experiment produced results that, for the most part, were not very different from what would be expected from Thomson's "plum pudding" model of the atom. Most alpha particles deflected only slightly if at all. However, an occasional alpha went missing. Searching for the missing alpha particles, Rutherford's students discovered they had deflected in unexpected directions. They had bounced far off to the side or nearly backwards. That led him to propose the existence of the nucleus.

While Geiger continued his detailed measurements, Rutherford assigned the task of looking for large-angle scattering to Ernest Marsden (1889–1970), another of his students. Marsden found that the missing alpha particles scattered to the left or right of the original detectors and a few even scattered backward. Rutherford described this result as "almost as incredible as if you had fired a 15-inch (38-centimeter) shell at a piece of tissue paper and it came back and hit you."

Rutherford explained his results with a new model of the atom. He envisioned an atom as a miniature solar system with electrical forces playing the role of gravity. Like the solar system, the atom is mostly empty space. Most of its mass is concentrated in a very small, positively charged **nucleus** (plural: nuclei) about one ten-thousandth of the size of the atom. In orbit around that minuscule but massive Sun are much tinier negatively charged planets: the electrons. Because the atoms are mostly empty space, most alpha particles passed through the foil without coming close enough to a nucleus to be scattered very much. Only on rare occasions would a fast-moving alpha particle make a nearly direct hit on a much heavier nucleus, which then scattered the alpha sideways or even backward.

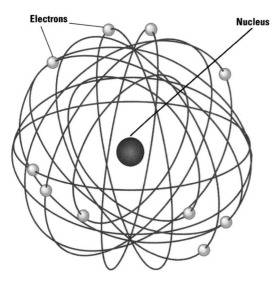

Electrons

Nucleus

The Planetary Model of the Atom. After discovering the nucleus, Rutherford proposed that atoms were like miniature solar systems held together by electric forces rather than gravity. Most of its mass was in its compact, positively charged nucleus, while tiny negatively charged electrons orbited that nucleus like a swarm of small planets.

Numbering the Periodic Table

But what was in the nucleus? Rutherford and other scientists concluded that the nucleus was composed of positive particles, which they called protons. Each nucleus contained as many protons as that atom had electrons. They also began to realize that the elements in the periodic table could be arranged in numerical order by how many protons or electrons they had. And this they called the **atomic number**.

It was not difficult experimentally to remove electrons from atoms, turning them into ions. Thus scientists decided that it was better to define atomic number by the positive charge in the nucleus. The atomic number thereby became the number of protons instead of the number of electrons. Hydrogen, the simplest atom with atomic number one, has a nucleus with a single proton. Helium, with atomic number two, has two protons, and so forth. However, the issue proved to be more complicated.

The atomic mass of hydrogen is one, but the atomic mass of helium is four. Other atoms reveal similar discrepancies. Lead, for example, has an atomic number of 82 and an atomic mass of approximately 207. Protons alone could not account for even half the mass of most nuclei. What else might be there?

Perhaps this extra mass could explain another problem in Rutherford's atomic model. If the nucleus contained only protons, they would repel each other with electric forces. Packed together in such a tiny space, that repulsive force would be enormous. Whatever else was in the nucleus to give it more mass would also have to exert an even larger attractive force to overcome the protons' electrical repulsion. Rutherford knew that he had just barely begun to understand the nucleus and the forces that act within it.

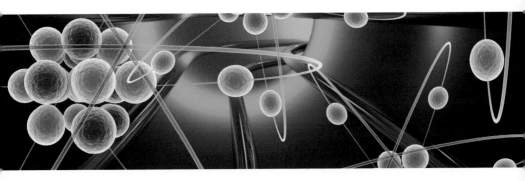

3 PARTICLES
Within the Nucleus

Rutherford was already famous when he discovered the nucleus. His studies of radioactivity had earned him the 1908 Nobel Prize in Chemistry for his careful measurements of alpha, beta, and gamma rays. He, along with his former colleague Soddy and other scientists, learned to identify different radioactive elements by distinct characteristics of their emissions. In that work, they realized that nature was succeeding where had failed: transforming one element into another. The process, which was called **transmutation**, hinted that atoms contained other particles besides electrons. Just as electrons were responsible for chemical reactions, those other particles were responsible for radioactivity and transmutation.

Once Rutherford, Geiger, and Marsden discovered the nucleus, it was clear that radioactivity originated within that small central region of an atom. Rutherford, and especially

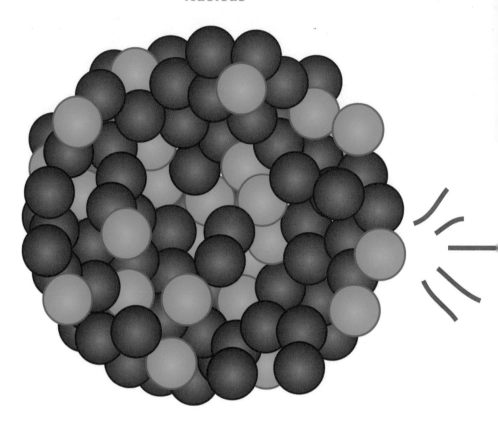

Soddy, began tracking the elements from their original form
to their new forms. They found that when a nucleus emits
an alpha particle, it loses four units of atomic mass while
its atomic number decreases by two. Nuclei that emit **beta
particles** do not change atomic mass, but their atomic numbers
increase by one unit. In both of those cases, an atom of one
element transmutes into an atom of a different element. The
new "daughter" atom is often radioactive, more so than its
"parent," so there is a chain of radioactive decay from one
atom to another.

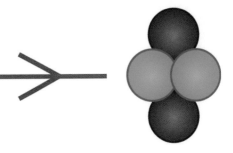

Alpha particle (2 protons, 2 neutrons)

Transmutation in Alpha Decay. Rutherford and Soddy described the process of radioactive decay as transmutation that produces a "daughter" nucleus from a "parent." In alpha decay, the daughter has an atomic number that is two less than the parent's and an atomic mass that is reduced by four. That led them to conclude that an alpha particle is a helium nucleus.

Rutherford and Soddy also discovered that several of the daughter atoms in different radioactive decay chains behaved the same way chemically, which meant that they have the same atomic numbers, yet their atomic masses were different. Soddy suggested calling such atoms isotopes (from the Greek for "equal place"). Chemists soon discovered that many non-radioactive atoms also had more than one isotopic form as well. To distinguish one isotope from another, they began denoting atoms by their chemical symbol and their atomic mass. Chlorine, for example, has naturally occurring

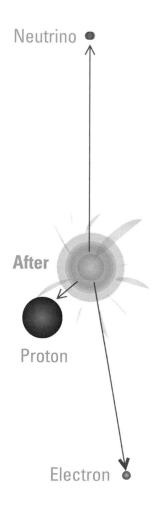

Neutrino

Before

Neutron about
to decay

After

Proton

Transmutation in Beta Decay. In beta decay, the daughter nucleus has an atomic number that is one greater than its parent and an atomic mass that is virtually unchanged. After Rutherford proposed that a nucleus contained neutrons as well as protons, he envisioned that a beta particle was the electron resulting from the decay of a neutron into a proton. That was not quite correct. In order to obey the law of conservation of energy, the emission of an additional particle called the neutrino was also necessary.

Electron

isotopes with atomic masses of 35 and 37. The more common of the two is Cl^{35}, which explains why chemists measure the atomic mass of natural chlorine as 35.47.

More Than Protons

Once Rutherford discovered the nucleus, he naturally drew on his work with radioactivity when considering what was inside nuclei. No one questioned that the hydrogen nucleus was a single proton that carried the same amount of positive charge

Chemistry vs. Alchemy

Before Rutherford discovered the nucleus, he did not realize that the radioactivity was coming from deep inside the atom or that transmutation was very different from alchemy and its scientific successor, chemistry. Chemical changes are related to the atoms' electrons and the bonds they form between atoms, but chemistry never changes atomic number or atomic mass. Radioactivity, however, comes from the within the nucleus and transforms one atom into another. Unfortunately for those people who hoped to achieve the alchemists' dream of transforming lead into gold, radioactive transformations went the other way, beginning with rare and valuable elements such as uranium and ending—often billions of years later—with much less valuable lead.

as the electron's negative charge. Rutherford's studies had shown that alpha particles were helium nuclei, which carried two units of positive charge but had an atomic mass of four units. Looking at the atoms that produced the radioactivity, some scientists suggested that the extra mass in a nucleus was due to extra protons plus an equal number of electrons. Rutherford didn't agree, and in 1920, a year after replacing the retiring J. J. Thomson as leader of the Cavendish Laboratory at Cambridge University, he explained it in this way.

An electron inside a nucleus would experience a powerful electrical attraction to any proton it would encounter and the pair would quickly bind together in a single, electrically neutral unit, a subatomic particle he called a **neutron**. He theorized that the alpha particles were made of four subatomic particles, two protons each with one unit of positive electric charge plus two uncharged neutrons.

Rutherford had already established that a radioactive atom that emits an alpha particle experiences a decrease of two in atomic number and four in atomic mass. Now he was saying that those decreases were due to a smaller helium nucleus—a unit of two protons and two neutrons—bursting out of the larger unstable nucleus of a radioactive atom. He explained beta emission as the result of the splitting of a neutron into a proton and an electron. Since electrons are so light, the new nucleus would have approximately the same atomic mass but its atomic number would increase by one.

Even scientists who agreed with Rutherford's theories wouldn't accept them without proof. "Show me neutrons," they would insist, and Rutherford set out to do just that. It took more than a decade, during which physicists devised many new devices and techniques to observe the paths of subatomic particles through matter, though not the particles themselves. Those techniques were very effective for revealing the passage of electrically charged particles, but the neutron, if it existed, would remain invisible.

Finally, in 1932, James Chadwick (1891–1974), one of Rutherford's colleagues at the Cavendish Laboratory, figured out a way to detect neutrons indirectly but convincingly. The basic structure and components of atoms as we now know them—positively charged nuclei of protons and neutrons carrying most of the mass while filling only about a ten-thousandth of the atom's diameter, surrounded by light electrons—had been established.

Other Revolutions in Physics

While Rutherford concentrated on the nucleus, two other revolutions in physics were also taking place:

James Chadwick (1891–1974). Detecting an electrically neutral particle like the neutron was a challenging problem. In 1932, Chadwick found a way to detect neutrons indirectly. His experiment is described in detail in *Understanding Neutrons* in this series.

Where Rutherford Was Not Quite Right

Rutherford's explanation of beta rays was not quite right. He was correct that a neutron within the nucleus transforms into a proton and an electron. But later research revealed that he had left something out. When the nucleus of a particular radioactive isotope nucleus emits an alpha particle, that alpha always carries the same amount of energy. That allows scientists to identify the isotope by the energy of its alpha particle. The same is true of gamma rays.

But beta rays are different. They can have any amount of energy up to a certain maximum. That caused a problem, because the scientific principle of conservation of energy was never violated in any other circumstance. Energy could change form, but it was never gained or lost. Einstein's famous equation $E = mc^2$ showed that mass was a form of energy. When a neutron transforms into a proton and an electron, the nucleus loses a small amount of mass that transforms into energy. The proton stays in place, but the electron leaves the nucleus as a beta particle and carries some of that energy with it.

Experiments showed that the energy the beta particle carried was never more than the lost mass. But it could be much less. To conserve energy, Wolfgang Pauli (1900–1958) proposed in 1930 that another particle was also emitted. That particle could not carry electric charge or have much mass, which made it very hard to detect. He called it the neutrino, for "little neutral one." The neutrino was a central part of a theory of beta decay published by Enrico Fermi (1901–1954) in 1933, and it was finally detected in 1956.

Enrico Fermi (1901–1954). Fermi developed a full theory to explain beta decay. Besides producing an electron (the beta particle), the decay process also led to the emission of a very light, electrically uncharged particle, the "little neutral one," or *neutrino* in Fermi's native Italian.

quantum mechanics and relativity. Together, they transformed our scientific understanding of matter and energy, and space and time. Albert Einstein had a hand in both. Amazingly, he published his groundbreaking ideas in both fields in 1905, the same year that his explanation of Brownian motion proved that atoms and molecules are real.

The most famous scientific equation of all time is probably Einstein's $E = mc^2$, which he wrote almost as an afterthought to his **theory of relativity**. Just as relativity uncovered surprising relationships between space and time, this equation expressed the unexpected fact that mass (m) and energy (E) are two sides of the same coin. They are measured in different units, so a conversion factor is needed to match them. Nature's conversion factor between mass and energy is the speed of light (c) squared, or multiplied by itself. As scientists began to measure the masses of protons, neutrons, and the nuclei of different isotopes, they began to see the power of that simple equation. For example, when a radioactive nucleus emits an alpha particle, the mass of the daughter nucleus plus the mass of the alpha particle add up to less than the original mass. The missing mass turns out to be exactly the energy carried by the alpha particle.

Einstein's third great idea of 1905, and the one that led to his winning the Nobel Prize in 1921, changed the relationship between matter and energy in another way. He looked at two puzzling recent discoveries. The first was the **photoelectric effect**, in which light could knock electrons free from metals but only if its frequency was high enough. The second was an odd idea developed a few years earlier by Max Planck (1858–1947) in his calculations of the **spectrum** (the mix of colors) produced by a hot body. Planck's equation depended on having light energy coming not in smooth waves like water, but in a stream of packets called quanta. He didn't believe that quanta were real, but they fixed a serious problem with his calculations. Einstein realized that the photoelectric effect was evidence that Planck's quanta, which later became known as **photons**, were real.

Other scientists soon recognized that all subatomic particles are quanta, just like photons, and they behave like waves at the atomic scale. They developed a new field called quantum mechanics that described the situation. For example, electrons in atoms had certain allowed wavelike states, each corresponding to a certain energy level specified by four "quantum numbers." Quantum mechanics worked spectacularly well for hydrogen, and when scientists imagined building larger atoms by adding more protons and electrons to them, they discovered something even better. The atoms had periodic properties. More than fifty years after Mendeleyev's dream, the periodic table made sense.

Quantum mechanics also changed the way science understood the basic forces of nature. For example, the laws of electromagnetism were recast in a new mathematical form called quantum electrodynamics, developed in the 1940s. These laws explain electromagnetic attraction and repulsion as the result of exchanging photons between electrically charged quanta, such as electrons and protons. In fact, in the quantum world, all forces are the result of such particle exchanges—and that takes us back into the nucleus. If protons repel one another by exchanging photons, what keeps the nucleus from blowing itself apart? There must be another force at work inside the nucleus, and it must have something to do with both protons and neutrons. That force is known

The Power of Nuclear Forces. The universe is comprised of billions or trillions of galaxies like this one, each containing billions or trillions of stars. Stars produce their vast amounts of light by nuclear processes that rely on the strong and weak nuclear forces.

as the **strong nuclear force**, or simply the **strong force**. (There's another force called the **weak nuclear force** that explains beta decay.)

The strong force must have some unusual properties. Unlike electromagnetism, which extends its influence a long way, the strong force must become insignificant beyond nuclear distances. Otherwise, nuclei of different atoms would be drawn together and the universe would collapse into one giant atom. It must be much more powerful than the electromagnetic force within the nucleus, yet there must be a limit to its power outside the nucleus so that particles are not crushed to nothingness.

Such a force can be understood by mathematical approaches that are similar to those used in quantum electrodynamics, with a few differences. Nucleons—protons and neutrons—attract through a property that physicists call color, the strong-force equivalent of electric charge, and instead of trading massless photons, they exchange particles called pi-mesons that have a mass of about 250 times that of an electron.

Of all the known forces in nature, the strong nuclear force is the most powerful of all. It is also very important in other ways. It is not only responsible for holding nuclei together, but it is also the source of the energy of the stars.

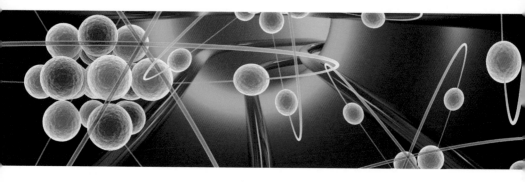

4 PROTONS
and Nuclear Fusion

Looking around us, we can find many different elements. Thus we rarely think about how different our world is from most of the universe. Except for hydrogen, most of the atoms on Earth are uncommon. To understand why that is so, we need to consider how the universe began.

The best current scientific understanding is that the universe burst into being 13.7 billion years ago in an event commonly called the big bang. It began as seething, expanding matter and high-energy photons. In a short time, most of that matter became the subatomic particles we now know so well, mostly protons, electrons, and neutrinos. Initially, it was too hot for atoms to form. As the universe then expanded and cooled, the subatomic particles joined to make atomic matter.

Element Factories. Everywhere we look in the universe, we see galaxies. This image shows a relatively close group of galaxies known as Hickson 44. If we study their light we can detect small amounts of most of the familiar elements on Earth. Most of those elements were not present immediately after the big bang. It took several generations of stars, powered by nuclear fusion, to produce all the elements heavier than lithium (atomic number 3).

Most of the atoms were hydrogen. Almost all the rest were helium, except for a tiny bit of lithium (atomic number 3). None of the atoms with heavier nuclei familiar to us on Earth—carbon, nitrogen, oxygen, aluminum, iron, and so forth—were anywhere to be found. Even today, most of the matter in the universe is hydrogen, and thus most of its mass is from protons. That is even true about our bodies, although they also contain plenty of neutrons.

Most of the atoms in our bodies are hydrogen, but those atoms are combined with heavier atoms in compounds, for example with oxygen in water. Those heavier atoms contribute most of our bodies' mass. Our bodies also need energy, extracted from plant and animal matter. That energy originally came to

Naming the Big Bang

Cosmology is an unusual science, since its subject is the whole universe. Although there are some competing ideas about the history of the cosmos, the most generally accepted one is called the big bang theory. The theory has its roots in the work of astronomer Edwin Hubble (1889–1953), who studied distant galaxies and discovered that, except for the very nearest ones, they were moving away from our own galaxy, the Milky Way. The farther they were from us, the faster they were receding.

Hubble published his interpretation of the results in 1929. His explanation, which came to be called Hubble's Law, was that the universe was expanding at a constant rate. Tracing that expansion back in time led to the conclusion at one point in the distant past, all the matter and energy in the universe was concentrated in a very tiny region. It began expanding and cooling to produce the cosmos we observe today.

Every theory has its critics, and one of the most important doubters was Fred Hoyle (1915–2001). Hoyle's competing theory described a universe in a steady state that grew by the slow but steady emergence of new matter throughout all space. During a 1949 interview on a BBC radio program, Hoyle used the phrase "big bang" to mock the idea that the universe began in an explosion. The name stuck.

Ironically, one of the best pieces of evidence supporting the big bang theory comes from a 1957 publication by Hoyle and four other scientists. In it, the scientists predicted the ratio of hydrogen, helium, and other elements that would emerge from the big bang

Giants of the Cosmos. In his study of distant galaxies in the 1920s, Edwin Hubble (*right*) discovered that the universe is expanding. His results have led to a theory that the cosmos as we see it now is the result of a single explosive event nearly 14 billion years ago. Noted astronomer Fred Hoyle never accepted that explanation. He developed a competing "steady state" theory and derided the idea of a massive explosion as "the big bang." The name, intended as an insult, stuck in the public's imagination.

and how much of the other elements would be forged later in the stars. Those predictions matched actual measurements so well that it would be hard to consider any other explanation—though Hoyle never stopped trying to come up with an alternative.

Earth from sunlight. So what do these facts have to do with protons? Everything!

The Sun is a star, and, besides making light, stars are the factories where nature has cooked its heavier nuclei. The cooking process is called nuclear **fusion**, and it begins with the most common nuclear raw material available in the universe: protons.

How Stars Create Heavier Elements

During the big bang, much of what happened was the opposite of what goes on in radioactive decay. For example, in beta decay, a nucleus emits a beta particle (an electron) and a neutrino when one of its neutrons gives up some of its mass to become a proton. To reverse the process and make a neutron from a proton, an electron, and a neutrino, those three particles would need to come together with at least as much energy as was released in the decay process.

In the early stages of the big bang, protons, electrons, and neutrinos appeared first. Everything was so close together and moving fast enough to make some neutrons. But the expansion was so rapid that the making of neutrons ended quickly, leaving most matter in the form of protons, electrons, and neutrinos.

Besides making neutrons, the early universe was also hot and dense enough to cook up a few other nuclei. For instance, some protons and neutrons paired off to form the nucleus of a heavier isotope of hydrogen with mass number 2 called deuterium (denoted as D or H^2). Two isotopes of helium also formed. The more common helium nucleus was the alpha particle (two protons and two neutrons or He^4), but helium nuclei with only one neutron (He^3) were also stable. Very small numbers of nuclei of other light elements also formed in the big bang. When the first burst of matter-creation ended, the nuclei picked up electrons. At that point, most matter in the universe consisted of hydrogen atoms and almost all the rest was helium atoms.

Once atoms formed, gravity could prevail over the more powerful electric force. Bare nuclei would repel each other electrically, but not neutral atoms. In some regions of the early universe, by pure chance, more atoms than average had formed. There, gravitational attraction began to draw

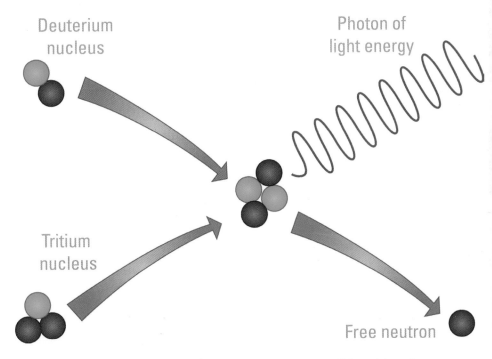

Deuterium nucleus

Photon of light energy

Tritium nucleus

Free neutron

Star Power. Stars produce their energy by nuclear fusion, or combining light nuclei to make heavier ones. This diagram shows one fusion process that happens inside the Sun: deuterium-tritium, or D-T fusion. Both D and T are heavy isotopes of hydrogen with one proton. D has one neutron and T has two neutrons. They combine to form a nucleus of helium-4 and a free neutron. Because the total mass after the reaction is less than before, the extra mass becomes energy, which is carried off as light.

the atoms together, slowly at first and then more rapidly. Eventually large numbers of atoms were coming together at high speed, sometimes heating up enough to strip away their electrons. Because of their high speed, not even electrical repulsion could stop the nuclei from getting close enough so that nuclear forces would take over. If circumstances were right, the nuclei would fuse, or join together.

Unlike the process that created neutrons from protons, electrons, and neutrinos in the early instants of the big bang, nuclear fusion events can sometimes release energy instead of absorbing it. That occurs when they make a particularly stable nucleus. For example, two deuterium nuclei (or deuterons) release energy when they fuse to form an alpha particle. Before and after the fusion event, there are two protons and two neutrons, but the alpha particle has less mass than the two deuterons. The difference in mass is released as energy.

Such fusion events are what powers stars such as the Sun, although the precise fusion reactions that take place are a bit more complicated than this example. Still, if gravity pulls enough hydrogen together in one place, fusion begins and continues until nearly all the protons have fused into alpha particles. While the star is "burning" its proton fuel, the outward pressure due to the heat counteracts the gravitational force that has been collapsing the matter.

When that fuel is finally used up, the collapse begins again, which raises the temperature of the star. Suddenly, there is enough energy to ignite other fusion events, such as the combination of three alpha particles into a carbon nucleus (C^{12}), which may fuse with another alpha particle to make an oxygen nucleus (O^{16}) at a still higher temperature. Those processes also release energy, but each step requires a higher temperature to ignite it. Depending on its size, each star stops

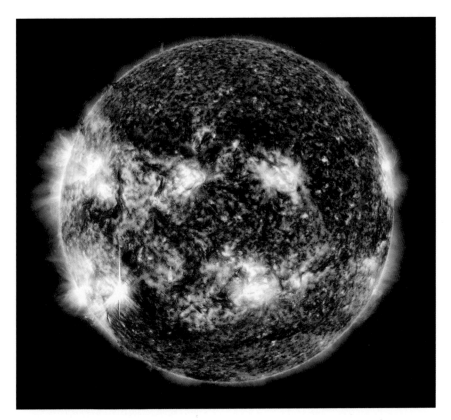

Seeing (Infra)Red. The Sun's nuclear fusion furnace produces energy as electromagnetic waves of many wavelengths. This infrared image shows solar features that might not be apparent in visible light.

all fusion at a different point, and becomes a slowing cooling cinder. For example, in about five or six billion years, our Sun will end up as a ball made mostly of hot carbon.

Larger stars follow other paths, but once a star is done fusing its nuclei into iron, additional fusion requires more energy than it produces. Iron's atomic number is only 26. So where did Earth get all its elements with much larger numbers of protons? To make those elements requires a powerful event known as a supernova explosion, which occurs only for the largest stars. Those stars have so much mass that gravity squeezes their nuclei together until they explode with great

Seeds of Future Worlds. When a supernova such as this one explodes, its intense energy can create the heaviest known elements. Ordinary stars can only fuse nuclei up to the size of iron, atomic number 26. All of Earth's heavier elements were made long ago in supernova explosions like this one. The formation of the Sun itself may have been triggered by a supernova explosion that sent a shock wave through a quiet cloud of dust, creating clumps of matter that then attracted each other to form a star and its planets.

violence. The event produces so much energy that it forces nuclei to fuse that would not ordinarily do so.

It is sometimes thought that the products of fusion would all be unstable and blow apart as soon as the pressure is released. Many of them are, but some are like water in a deep well on top of a mountain. Once the water is in the well, you need a lot of energy to pump it out so it can run down to the valley. A few nuclei are radioactive—unstable but lasting a long time. They are like water in a shallower mountaintop well where severe storms come by from time to time. If you wait long enough, a storm is sure to strike and blow the water out.

Fusion Research and Technology

Understanding the nuclear processes in stars took a lot of research, and people involved in research often think about ways they can apply their discoveries. For instance, fusion energy has already been used in fearsome military weapons known as "hydrogen bombs" or "thermonuclear devices." Might there be a way to make an electric power plant operating on the same principle? It would be like capturing the energy of the stars in a bottle.

Engineers have been trying to build fusion reactors for electric power for more than fifty years. The biggest problem has been finding a bottle to contain the super-hot gases. Since the fusing nuclei are electrically charged, they respond to magnetic fields, but even a slight instability is enough to disrupt the process before enough fusion energy is released. It takes electrical energy to make the powerful magnetic

Nuclear Fusion on Earth. The world's most powerful weapons, called thermonuclear devices, create powerful bursts of nuclear fusion energy. These are many times more powerful than the bombs that used nuclear fission (splitting of heavy nuclei) that were dropped on Japan to end World War II. This image shows an American test explosion of a thermonuclear bomb. No aboveground American nuclear weapons tests have taken place since 1963.

fields needed. So far, the most successful devices have only succeeded in producing more energy than it takes to run the reactor for a very short time, and at a great cost.

Another fusion power technique is called inertial confinement, and it avoids the need to create a powerful magnetic field. Instead, it blasts a pellet of hydrogen-rich material on all sides with a laser or similar intense energy source, hoping to create a situation that likens to the process by which material is drawn inward by a star's gravity. The object is to create enough fusion reactions quickly before the heat blows the material outward again. It seems like a good idea, but so far it has been very difficult to achieve in practice.

Pieces of Protons

As scientists investigated subatomic particles and new forces, such as the strong and weak nuclear force, they have created machines that make beams of protons. These beams have a number of uses, including the treatment of some forms of cancer and the detection of very small amounts of certain elements in a sample of material. Probably the most interesting use is what happens when proton beams are accelerated to nearly the speed of light and then allowed to collide. The result is a shower of new and very unusual particles that reveal inner secrets of matter that might have surprised Ernest Rutherford even more than the discovery of the nucleus did.

One of those surprises is that, like atoms, protons and neutrons are not indivisible. They contain even smaller particles called **quarks**. Quarks stick together so tightly that they can never be detected separately, though scattering experiments can reveal their presence just as Rutherford's experiments showed that atoms have nuclei.

Electricity from Fusion? Nuclear fusion promises to be an important source of electrical energy for the future. But despite years of research, it remains difficult to ignite a fusion reaction that can be contained and controlled. These German workers are building the main fusion chamber of the Wendelstein 7-X experimental fusion reactor in Greifswald, which was nearing completion in 2015.

There's a lot you can learn about both quarks and the history of machines that create high-energy beams of protons or other particles. Fortunately, you don't have to go far to do that. This series includes books about both quarks and the particle accelerators that led to their discovery.

Glossary

alchemy A field of study that preceded chemistry, through which many people hoped to transform less valuable metals into gold but never succeeded.

alpha particle or **alpha ray** A helium nucleus that is emitted from some radioactive elements.

atom The smallest bit of matter than can be identified as a certain chemical element.

atomic mass or **atomic weight** The mass of a particular atom compared to a standard. For a particular isotope, that value is approximately the number of protons plus the number of neutrons in its nucleus. For a naturally occurring element, that value is approximately the number of protons plus the average number of neutrons in the nuclei of naturally occurring isotopes.

atomic number The number of protons in the nucleus of an atom, which determines its chemical identity as an element.

beta particle or **beta ray** An electron that is emitted from some radioactive elements.

Brownian motion The jiggling motion of a piece of dust or pollen suspended in a fluid, first observed by Robert

Brown and eventually shown by Albert Einstein to demonstrate the existence of atoms and molecules.

compound A substance made of only one kind of molecule that consists of more than one kind of atom. For example, water is made of molecules that contain two atoms of hydrogen and one atom of oxygen (H_2O).

electromagnetic An adjective to describe a fundamental force of nature, or property of matter and energy, that includes electricity, magnetism, and electromagnetic waves, such as light.

electron A very light subatomic particle (the first to be discovered) that carries negative charge and is responsible for the chemical properties of matter.

element A substance made of only one kind of atom.

emission Sending out something that has been produced, such as the emission of an alpha, beta, or gamma ray from a radioactive atom.

fusion The joining of two nuclei to form a new nucleus.

gamma ray A high-energy photon that is emitted from some radioactive elements.

molecule The smallest bit of matter that can be identified as a certain chemical compound.

neutron A subatomic particle with neutral electric charge found in the nucleus of atoms.

nucleus The very tiny and positively charged central part of an atom that carries most of its mass.

periodic table of the elements An arrangement of the elements in rows and columns by increasing atomic number, first proposed by Dmitry Mendeleyev, in which elements in the same column have similar chemical properties.

photoelectric effect A phenomenon in which light can, under some circumstances, knock electrons out of atoms.

photon A particle that carries electromagnetic energy, such as light energy.

proton A subatomic particle with positive electric charge found in the nucleus of atoms.

quantum mechanics A field of physics developed to describe the relationships between matter and energy that accounts for the dual wave-particle nature of both.

quark A sub-subatomic particle that exists in several forms that combine to make protons, neutrons, and some other subatomic particles.

radioactivity A property of unstable atoms that causes them to emit alpha, beta, or gamma rays.

scattering An experimental technique used to detect the shape or properties of an unseen object by observing how other objects deflect from it.

spectrum The mixture of colors contained within a beam of light, or the band produced when those colors are spread out by a prism or other device that separates the colors from each other.

strong nuclear force or **strong force** A fundamental force of nature that acts to hold the protons and neutrons in a nucleus together.

theory of relativity A theory developed by Albert Einstein that dealt with the relationship between space and time. Its most famous equation ($E = mc^2$) described the relationship between mass and energy.

transmutation The transformation of one element to another by a change in its nucleus, such as by alpha or beta emission.

weak nuclear force or **weak force** A fundamental force of nature that is responsible for beta decay of a radioactive nucleus.

For Further Information

Books

Bortz, Fred. *The Big Bang Theory: Edwin Hubble and the Origin of the Universe*. New York: Rosen, 2014.

———. *The Periodic Table of Elements and Dmitry Mendeleyev*. New York: Rosen, 2014.

———. *Physics: Decade by Decade*. Twentieth-Century Science. New York: Facts On File, 2007.

Challoner, Jack. *The Elements: The New Guide to the Building Blocks of Our Universe*. London: Carlton Books, 2012.

Green, Dan, and Simon Basher. *Extreme Physics*. New York: Kingfisher, 2013.

Hagler, Gina. *Discovering Quantum Mechanics*. New York: Rosen, 2015.

Hollar, Sherman. *Electronics*. New York: Britannica Educational Services, 2012.

Marsico, Katie. *Key Discoveries in Physical Science.* Minneapolis, MN: Lerner Publications, 2015.

Morgan, Sally. *From Greek Atoms to Quarks:* Discovering Atoms. New York: Heinemann Publishing, 2008.

Websites

American Institute of Physics
Center for the History of Physics
www.aip.org/history-programs/physics-history

This site includes several valuable online exhibits from the history of physics, including The Discovery of the Electron and Rutherford's Nuclear World.

The Nobel Foundation Prizes for Physics
www.nobelprize.org/nobel_prizes/physics

Learn more about past Nobel Prize winners, including J. J. Thomson, Ernest Rutherford, Louis de Broglie, Albert Einstein, and George Paget Thomson. Each entry includes quick biographical facts and brief summaries of their award-winning contributions to physics.

The Science Museum (UK)
www.sciencemuseum.org.uk

This site includes the online exhibit Atomic Firsts, which tells the story of Ernest Rutherford, J. J. Thomson and his son George Paget Thomson, who also won the Nobel Prize for his experiment that proved the existence of de Broglie's predicted electron waves.

Museums and Institutes

American Chemical Society (ACS)
1155 Sixteenth Street NW
Washington, DC 20036
(800) 227-5558
portal.acs.org/portal/acs/corg/content

Chartered by the US Congress, the ACS is one of the world's leading sources of trustworthy and accurate scientific information.

American Institute of Physics
Center for the History of Physics
One Physics Ellipse
College Park, MD 20740
(301) 209-3165
www.aip.org/history-programs/physics-history

The Center for History of Physics houses a research library, a photo archive, and has created numerous online resources in all areas of physics, including Rutherford's Nuclear World.

Ernest Rutherford Collection
Room 111 Ernest Rutherford Physics Building
McGill University
3600 rue University
Montréal, QC H3A 2T8
Canada
(514) 398-6490
www.mcgill.ca/historicalcollections/departmental/ernest-rutherford

On permanent display at the Rutherford Museum is the apparatus used by Nobel Prize winner Ernest Rutherford when he was professor of experimental physics at McGill from 1898 to 1907.

Lederman Science Education Center
Fermilab MS 777
Box 500
Batavia, IL 60510
(630) 840-8258
ed.fnal.gov/lsc/lscvideo/index.shtml

Visit the Lederman Science Education Center and explore the science and history of subatomic particles.

Ontario Science Centre
770 Don Mills Road
Toronto, ON M3C 1T3
Canada
(416) 696-1000
www.ontariosciencecentre.ca

The Ontario Science Centre is Canada's leading science and technology museum. Its programs and exhibits aim to inspire a lifelong journey of curiosity, discovery, and action to create a better future for the planet.

Index

Page numbers in **boldface** are illustrations. Entries in **boldface** are glossary terms.

About the Authors

Science educator and consultant **B. H. Fields** has worked behind the scenes in the publishing industry since the mid-1980s, specializing in books and articles on the physical sciences and technology for middle grades.

Award-winning children's author **Fred Bortz** spent the first twenty-five years of his working career as a physicist, gaining experience in fields as varied as nuclear reactor design, automobile engine control systems, and science education. He earned his PhD at Carnegie Mellon University, where he also worked in several research groups from 1979 through 1994. He has been a full-time writer since 1996.